THE ILLUSTRATED

TEXAS
DICTIONARY

of the

ENGLISH LANGUAGE

VOLUME ONE

by Jim Everhart

With 49 photographs of the author
by Thaine Manske

CLIFFS NOTES, INC. • LINCOLN, NEBRASKA 68501

EX TEXAS LIBRIS

★

Nobody enjoys a joke on himself
more than a Texan. This book
has been done in good fun to share
one small facet of Texas humor
with you.

JIM EVERHART

Houston, Texas

ISBN 0-8220-1477-7

yawl — the pronoun of the second person plural. "Good to see *yawl*."

ward — a unit of language consisting of one or more spoken sounds. "Pardon me, could ah have a *ward* with yawl?"

lahr — a prevaricator; one who tells lies. "Are yew callin' me a *lahr?*"

watt — the lightest of colors. "Yew look *watt* as a sheet."

riot — correct or proper. "That's jes as *riot* as rain."

often — so as to be no longer supported or attached. "Now stan still so ah can shoot that apple *often* yore had."

barley — only, just, no more than. "Ah can jes *barley* open mah eyes."

pour — having little or no means of support. "Them folks is downriot *pour*."

blond — without sight.
"Love is *blond*."

lacked — was on the verge of or came close to. "Ah *lacked* to died laughin'."

main — of ugly disposition,
nasty. "That there is one *main* man."

felons — a substance used to close the cavities in teeth. "When ah open mah mouth real wad yawl can see mah two *felons*."

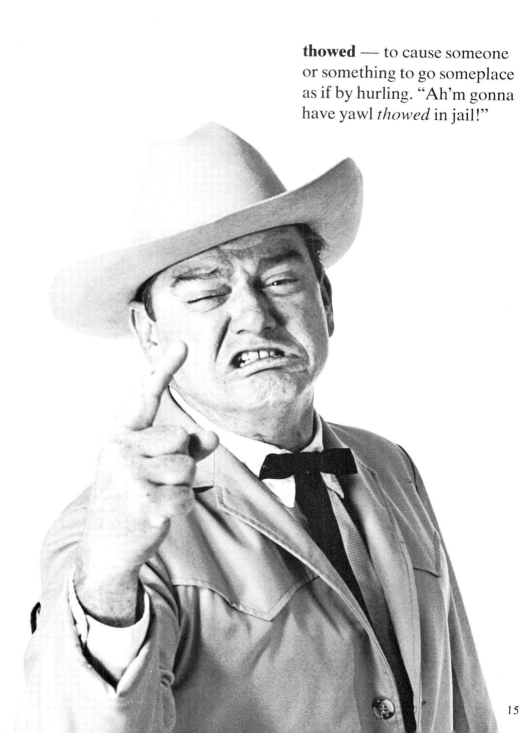

thowed — to cause someone or something to go someplace as if by hurling. "Ah'm gonna have yawl *thowed* in jail!"

15

rum — a portion of space within a building. "Ah got to go to the rest*rum*."

cheer — in this place or spot. "Yawl come riot *cheer* this minute!"

lard — the deity. "*Lard* only knows what happened."

beggar — larger as in size, height, width, amount, etc. "The *beggar* they come the harder they fall!"

thang — a material object without life or consciousness. "That don't main a *thang*."

prior — a devout petition to an object of worship. "Don't never say a *prior* with your hat on."

suede — dear, beloved,
precious. "Ain't that
jes too *suede* for wards?"

larry — wary, suspicious. "Ah would be *larry* of that if ah was yew."

prod — a high opinion of one's own dignity, importance, etc. "Ah take *prod* in mah work."

far — to discharge a firearm.
"Stop or ah'm gonna *far!*"

tarred — exhausted. "Boy, am ah *tarred!*"

they — the objective and dative case of thou. "Mah country tis of *they,* suede land of liberty, of *they* ah sang . . ."

hem — objective case of he. "Ah drawed mah gun on *hem*."

owe — an overwhelming feeling of reverence, admiration, fear, etc. "That there is one thang ah stand in *owe* of."

thote — the passage in the neck from the mouth to the stomach. "Ah got a sore *thote*."

sighting — arousing or
stirring up emotions.
"That was one beg,
sighting card game."

heidi — an expression of greeting. *"Heidi,* neighbor!"

sect — afflicted with ill health or disease. "Ah feel *sect* to mah stomach."

small — to assume a facial expression indicating pleasure. "*Small* and the whole world *smalls* with yew."

consarned — interested or participating. "Yawl ain't *consarned* in this no way!"

harket — going to the barber. "Mah hat never fits after ah get a *harket*."

drank — any liquid taken into the mouth and swallowed. "How 'bout a lil *drank?*"

squire — honest and above board. "Everythang here is fire and *squire*."

ails — other than the person or things implied. "Ah only done what anybody *ails* would do."

fair — a distressing emotion aroused by impending danger, evil, etc. "The only thang we have to *fair* is *fair* itsef."

tom — any specific point in a day, a month, a year. "How come yawl ain't never on *tom?*"

air — the organ of hearing in man. "Ah got a *air*ache."

truss — reliance on integrity.
"Don't yawl *truss* me?"

43

mere — a reflecting surface. "Ah jes hate to look at mahsef in the *mere*."

hep — to render assistance. "Ain't nobody gonna *hep* me?"

rang — to twist
forcibly. "Ah'm gonna
rang yore neck."

farfanger — the first finger next to the thumb. "Ah'm holdin' mah nose 'twixt mah thumb an *farfanger*."

Markin — a citizen of the United States. "Ah am a *Markin*."